B
S 89A2

DETROIT PUBLIC   P9-DKF-428

3 5674 03673269 2

CHASE BRANCH LIBRARY
17731 W. SEVEN MILE RD.
DETROIT, MI 48235
578-8002

CH

A Picture Book of Harriet Beecher Stowe

by David A. Adler • illustrated by Colin Bootman

CHASE BRANCH LIBRARY
17731 W. SEVEN MILE RD.
DETROIT, MI 48235
578-8002

OCT - - 2003

Holiday House / New York

Text copyright © 2003 by David A. Adler
Illustrations copyright © 2003 by Colin Bootman
All Rights Reserved
Printed in the United States of America
www.holidayhouse.com
First Edition

Library of Congress Cataloging-in-Publication Data

Adler, David A.
A picture book of Harriet Beecher Stowe / David A. Adler; illustrated by Colin Bootman.—1st ed.
p. cm.—(Picture book biography)
Summary: Details the life and achievements of abolitionist Harriet Beecher Stowe
whose book, *Uncle Tom's Cabin*, is said to have started the Civil War.
Includes biographical references.
ISBN 0-8234-1646-1 (hardcover)
1. Stowe, Harriet Beecher, 1811–1896—Juvenile literature. 2. United States—
History—Civil War, 1861–1865—Literature and the war—Juvenile literature.
3. Authors, American—19th century—Biography—Juvenile literature. 4. Abolitionists—
United States—Biography—Juvenile literature. [1. Stowe, Harriet Beecher, 1811–1896.
2. Authors, American. 3. Abolitionists. 4. Women—Biography.]
I. Bootman, Colin, ill. II. Title.

PS2956.A64 2003
813'.3—dc21
[B]
2002027626

To Claire Counihan,
An ever-cheerful
and very talented designing woman
D. A. A.

With many thanks
to Sherri Axelred, Leia Gorban,
and Melissa Ennen
C. B.

In 1862 President Abraham Lincoln met Harriet Beecher Stowe. He shook her hand, it was reported, and said, "So this is the little lady who made this big war."

Harriet Beecher Stowe had written *Uncle Tom's Cabin*, a best-selling book. Many people felt her book stirred people to hate slavery and fight the Civil War.

Harriet Beecher Stowe was born in Litchfield, Connecticut, on June 14, 1811. She was the seventh of nine children, five sons and four daughters, of Roxana and Lyman Beecher.

Harriet's mother was a smart, quiet woman who loved books. But Harriet hardly knew her. In 1816 Roxana Beecher died of tuberculosis. Harriet was just five years old.

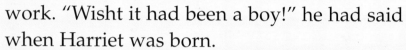

Lyman Beecher was a fiery-tongued minister.
He was a high-spirited, demanding father, and
wanted sons. The Reverend Beecher planned
to train them to be preachers to continue his
work. "Wisht it had been a boy!" he had said
when Harriet was born.

Soon after Roxana died, Lyman Beecher married Harriet Porter, "a beautiful lady, very fair," according to her stepdaughter Harriet, "a woman of great personal elegance." But she was also "naturally hard, correct, exact, and exacting." Lyman and his second wife had three children.

Harriet Beecher was a small, frail girl, quiet and shy. At times she seemed to be in her own dream world. At other times she was alert, alive with energy. Harriet loved to read. After she found an old copy of *The Arabian Nights* in a barrel that held her father's speeches, she read it again and again.

In 1824 thirteen-year-old Harriet moved thirty miles away, to Hartford, Connecticut, to attend the Hartford Female Seminary. It was run by her older sister Catharine.

Harriet loved to write. While she was at school,
she decided she had a talent for it and planned to use
it for good. "I do not mean to live in vain," she wrote
to her brother.

Harriet had a good mind and a great memory. By the time she was sixteen, she was teaching at the school. Many of her students were her own age.

In 1832 Lyman Beecher took a job as president of Lane Theological Seminary in Cincinnati, Ohio, and his family moved west. Connecticut and Ohio were free states. Slavery was not allowed. But slavery was allowed in Kentucky, which is just across the river from Ohio.

At first Harriet read newspaper accounts of slavery. "Passing along the wharf," began an editorial in the Cincinnati *Journal* soon after Harriet arrived there, was "the steamboat *Emigrant*." Loaded on board was a "cargo" of slaves, "bought in Virginia and Kentucky," to be sold farther south. The author of the editorial wrote of the "ocean of tears" the slave traders "have caused to flow." He wrote of the "broad stream the blood which their merciless thongs have drawn from human flesh."

In Cincinnati Harriet saw advertisements posted for runaway slaves with rewards promised for their return. There were also rewards promised for killers of certain Abolitionists—outspoken enemies of slavery.

Then, in 1833, during her summer break from teaching at the seminary, Harriet saw slaves at work. She saw them mistreated by their slaveholders. The visit made a deep impression on young Harriet Beecher.

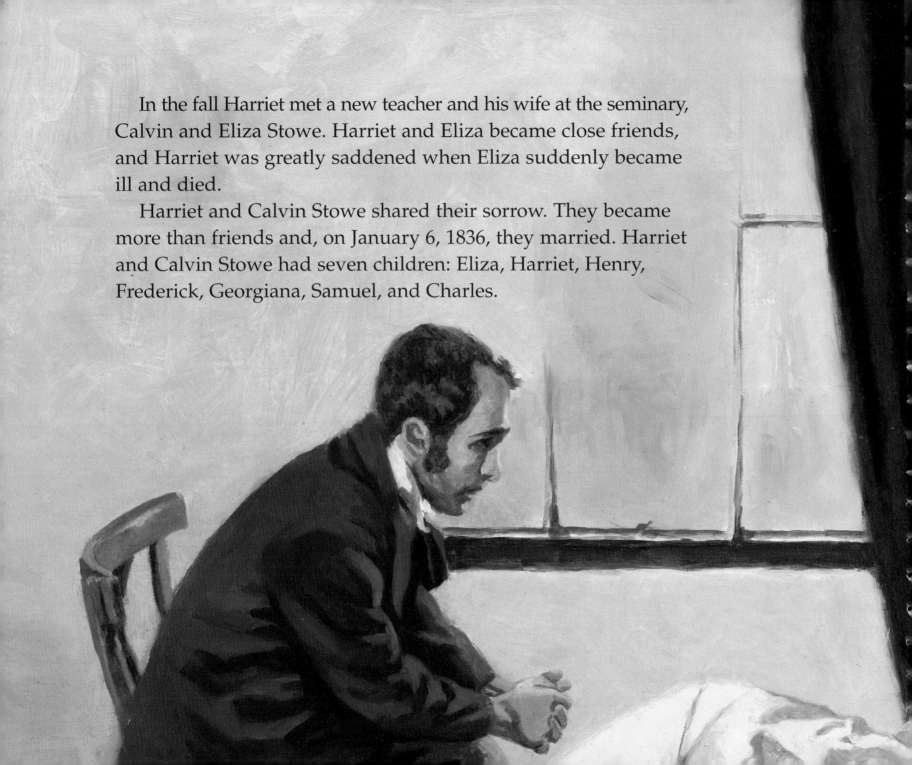

In the fall Harriet met a new teacher and his wife at the seminary, Calvin and Eliza Stowe. Harriet and Eliza became close friends, and Harriet was greatly saddened when Eliza suddenly became ill and died.

Harriet and Calvin Stowe shared their sorrow. They became more than friends and, on January 6, 1836, they married. Harriet and Calvin Stowe had seven children: Eliza, Harriet, Henry, Frederick, Georgiana, Samuel, and Charles.

At times they were close. "If you were not already my dearly beloved husband," Harriet once wrote to him, "I would surely fall in love with you." And at times they seemed like a poor match.

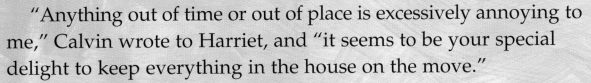

"Anything out of time or out of place is excessively annoying to me," Calvin wrote to Harriet, and "it seems to be your special delight to keep everything in the house on the move."

He also complained, "When your mind is on any particular point, it is your nature to feel and act as if that were the only thing in the world." For Harriet, that "only thing in the world" was often her writing.

Harriet wrote a geography textbook, stories, and articles for newspapers and magazines. In 1843 her first book, a collection of her stories, was published.

Calvin encouraged her writing. "My dear," he wrote to her when she was in New York, "you must be a literary woman. It is so written in the book of fate."

In 1850 Calvin took a teaching job at Bowdoin College and the Stowes moved to Brunswick, Maine.

The next year Harriet began a story called *Uncle Tom's Cabin*, about Tom, an old slave, and his evil slaveholder, Simon Legree. She wrote it in weekly installments for the *National Era*, an antislavery newspaper. At first, she thought she could finish it in three or four installments, but it took her forty weeks to complete. In 1852 it was published as a book.

In the story, Simon Legree wanted Tom to tell him where two runaway slaves were hiding. Tom refused and was beaten severely. "I'll count every drop of blood there is in you," Legree told Tom, "and take 'em, one by one, till ye give up!" Tom was beaten to death.

"I forgive ye," were Tom's dying words to Legree. "I forgive ye, with all my heart!"

UNCLE TOM'S
CABIN

The book was an immediate best-seller. Millions of
readers felt the horrors of slavery through the lives
of Tom, Eliza, and others in *Uncle Tom's Cabin*. People
who had perhaps hardly thought about the injustices of
slavery now hated it.

Surely the feelings stirred up by *Uncle Tom's Cabin*
helped elect President Lincoln. Harriet Beecher
Stowe's book was one of the causes of the Civil War.

Harriet Beecher Stowe wrote other books, articles, stories, and poems, but none of them had the power of *Uncle Tom's Cabin*.

In 1852 the Stowes moved to Andover, Massachusetts, after Calvin took a job there as a professor at the Andover Theological Seminary. In 1863 Calvin retired and the family moved to Hartford, Connecticut.

Calvin Stowe died in 1886. After that, Harriet was hardly seen outside her house. She died on July 1, 1896.

Small, frail-looking Harriet Beecher Stowe, the "little lady," awakened the nation to a terrible injustice. She helped shape the destiny of the American people.

AUTHOR'S NOTES

Tom, the hero of Stowe's book, is certainly not a role model. Because of his eagerness for approval, some people consider the book racist. But whatever the feelings are about Tom, the book did play an important role in ending slavery in the United States.

In 1853 it was reported that in its first year, more than 300,000 copies of *Uncle Tom's Cabin* were sold in the United States.

In the 1860s senators William Seward of New York and Charles Sumner of Massachusetts said Abraham Lincoln owed his nomination and election as president to *Uncle Tom's Cabin*.

In 1889 Kirk Munroe wrote in his book *Lives and Deeds of Our Self-Made Men* that Harriet Beecher Stowe stood in the "foremost rank of famous women," and that she had shaped "the destiny of the American people."

IMPORTANT DATES

1811	Born in Litchfield, Connecticut, on June 14.
1816	Mother, Roxana Foote Beecher, died of tuberculosis.
1824	Attended her sister's Hartford Female Seminary.
1832	Moved with her family to Cincinnati, Ohio.
1836	Married Calvin Stowe.
1850	Moved with family to Brunswick, Maine.
1851–1852	*Uncle Tom's Cabin* first published as a serialized story and as a book in 1852.
1852	Family moved to Andover, Massachusetts.
1862	Met President Abraham Lincoln.
1863	Family moved to Hartford, Connecticut.
1896	Died in Hartford, Connecticut, on July 1.

SELECTED BIBLIOGRAPHY

Hedrick, Joan D. *Harriet Beecher Stowe: A Life*. New York: Oxford University Press, 1994.

Johnston, Joanna. *Runaway to Heaven: The Story of Harriet Beecher Stowe*. New York: Doubleday, 1963.

Stowe, Harriet Beecher. *Uncle Tom's Cabin*. New York: Coward-McCann, 1929.

Wilson, Forrest. *Crusader in Crinoline: The Life of Harriet Beecher Stowe*. Philadelphia: Lippincott, 1941.

FURTHER READING

Bland, Celia. *Harriet Beecher Stowe*. Philadelphia: Chelsea House, 1993.

Fritz, Jean. *Harriet Beecher Stowe and the Beecher Preachers*. New York: Putnam, 1994.

Gelletly, LeeAnn. *Harriet Beecher Stowe*. Philadelphia: Chelsea House, 2001.

Johnston, Johanna. *Harriet and the Runaway Book*. New York: Harper, 1977.

Johnston, Norma. *Harriet: The Life of Harriet Beecher Stowe*. New York: Four Winds Press, 1994.

WEB SITES

www.harrietbeecherstowecenter.org
www.ohiohistory.org/places/stowe